Computer

Exp

Computer Terminology Explained

by

I. D. Poole
B.Sc.(Eng.), C.Eng., M.I.E.E.

BERNARD BABANI (publishing) LTD
THE GRAMPIANS
SHEPHERDS BUSH ROAD
LONDON W6 7NF
ENGLAND

PLEASE NOTE

Although every care has been taken with the production of this book to ensure that any projects, designs, modifications and/or programs etc. contained herein, operate in a correct and safe manner and also that any components specified are normally available in Great Britain, the Publishers do not accept responsibility in any way for the failure, including fault in design, of any project, design, modification or program to work correctly or to cause damage to any other equipment that it may be connected to or used in conjunction with, or in respect of any other damage or injury that may be so caused, nor do the Publishers accept responsibility in any way for the failure to obtain specified components.

Notice is also given that if equipment that is still under warranty is modified in any way or used or connected with home-built equipment then that warranty may be void.

© 1984 BERNARD BABANI (publishing) LTD

First Published – October 1984

British Library Cataloguing in Publication Data
Poole, I. D.
    Computer terminology explained.—(BP148)
    1. Computers—Dictionaries
    2. Electronic data processing—Dictionaries
    I. Title
    001.64'03'21   QA76.15

ISBN 0 85934 123 2

Printed and Bound in Great Britain by Cox & Wyman Ltd, Reading

Introduction

Over the past few years the home computer has become a commonplace item and people who until recently have never had access to a computer are finding they can now easily possess one. Looking through the shops, and in the computer magazines it can be seen that there is an exceedingly large selection of computers and also their various enhancements and peripherals. All of these are available at very reasonable prices. Whilst the boom in computer hardware sales has grown there has also been a corresponding growth in software sales, as well as in magazines and other computer literature. Very often this literature will contain a whole new realm of terms which is peculiar to the computer business and confusing to someone not familiar with it.

Unfortunately, this computer jargon can very easily set a barrier against people understanding some of the concepts and ideas surrounding computers. In addition to this it can give the impression that computer programming is only for an elite few, which is not true.

This book aims to set out definitions for most of the terms which should be encountered by the home computer enthusiast. In addition to this many terms have been included which are more easily used in connection with mini computers or the larger mainframe systems and this has been done so that an overall selection of terms is presented here.

I. D. Poole

Contents

Glossary of Computer Terminology

A

Absolute Addressing
A method of addressing locations within the computer's memory in which the actual address is stated.

Absolute Value
The value of a number taken without any regard for its sign. For example, the absolute value of 10 is 10 and of −15 is 15.

Access Time
The time interval taken between a request for data and its retrieval from a storage medium.

Accumulator
A holding register within the ALU (Arithmetic Logic Unit) which derives its name from its major function of adding and holding numbers.

Acknowledge
A signal given as part of a handshaking protocol to indicate that a section of information has been received and the receiver is ready for the next section.

Ada
A high-level computer language.

A/D Converter
An analogue-to-digital converter. An electronic circuit which converts analogue values such as voltage into a digital form.

Adder
A unit whose output is the addition of its inputs. Although there are normally only two inputs there can be more.

Address
A number which is used to specify the location of a particular item. An address may refer to a device on a bus or more commonly to a location within a computer's memory.

Addressing Mode
The particular method in which a computer refers to a location within its memory. There are several different ways in which memory locations may be addressed: absolute; immediate; direct and index addressing are a few examples.

Algol
A high-level language which was developed in Europe at about the same time Fortran was developed in the USA. It is a language which is particularly suited to solving mathematical problems. Its name is derived from the words ALGOrithmic Language because it enables problems to be solved by stating their algorithms as a set of computer statements.

Algorithm
A logical sequence of events containing defined steps for solving a problem.

Alphameric
A shortened form of Alphanumeric.

Alphanumeric
A character which is either a letter or a number.

ALU
Arithmetic Logic Unit.

American Standard Code
for Information Interchange
A numerical code used to represent letters, numbers and other functions within a computer, and when communicating between a computer and its peripherals. Although other codes are sometimes used, this one has gained most popularity. *See* Appendix 1.

Analog(ue)
A system or a circuit is said to be analogue if the variables within it are continuously variable unlike a digital system in which all values are represented by numbers and have to vary by steps, however small.

Analogue Computer
A computer which uses analogue techniques to perform its calculations. This is most often accomplished by representing any variables as analogue voltages within the system and using special electronic circuits to add, subtract, multiply, differentiate, etc. the signals. However, analogue computers are rarely used these days as digital ones are considerably more flexible, powerful and easy to use.

AND
A logical function from which a logical 1 or true output is obtained if the two input bits are a logical 1 or true, otherwise the output is 0 or false.

AND Gate
An electronic circuit which provides an AND function.

APL
A computer language designed for use mainly with time-sharing terminals and it has many powerful features. Its name is derived from the words "A Programming Language".

Application Program
A program which has been written to enable the computer to perform a specific task or fulfil a specific application.

Architecture
The architecture of a computer refers to the way in which the hardware, i.e., the registers, processor, memory, etc., of the machine has been designed and the way it all interconnects.

Argument
This is the variable used by a function to evaluate the value of that function. For example, in sin (x), x is the argument.

Arithmetic Logic Unit
The section of the processor which performs the arithmetic functions of addition and subtraction, logic functions and the shifting of numbers.

Arithmetic Shift
An arithmetic shift has the effect of multiplying or dividing a number by the base of the number once for every place shifted. A shift towards the left multiplies and to the right divides the number.

ASCII
See American Standard Code for Information Interchange.

Assembler
The assembler within a computer system is the software which converts a program written in assembly language into machine code instructions.

Assembly Language
This is a low-level language which makes machine code more easy to read by representing individual machine code instructions in a symbolic form. Once written, a program in assembly language requires assembling, i.e., converting to machine code before it can be executed.

Assignment Statement
An instruction or statement which gives a value to, or alters the value of a variable.

Asynchronous
A system is said to be asynchronous if it does not require an external timing source or clock for its operation.

B

Background

This can refer to a form of processing where a program or job takes a low priority and it will be run when there are no other jobs to be run. The term can also be used to describe the program or job itself.

Backup

A term used for a second copy of a disk or other storage medium made in case the first one becomes corrupted. A backup should be made wherever possible in case of a head crash or other form of data corruption.

Backus Naur

A form in which the syntax of a computer language may be described.

Base

The base of a numbering system is its radix, and it is equal to the number of characters used in the system e.g., ten for the decimal system (0 to 9) and two for the binary system (0 and 1).

BASIC

Beginners All-purpose Symbolic Instruction Code. A high-level language used on most microcomputer systems. Its advantages are that it is easy to learn and use.

Baud

This is a term used when referring to rates of data transmission, where in most cases one baud corresponds to one bit per second. The name is derived from Baudot who did a great amount of work in early communications systems.

BCD
See Binary Coded Decimal.

Binary
A numbering system which uses the base two. As it requires only two digits (0 and 1) it is used within digital computers because the two digits can be represented by the presence or absence of a voltage.

Binary Coded Decimal
A system where decimal numbers are represented in a binary form with each decimal digit being represented by four bits. Although a four-bit binary number can represent numbers in the range 0 to 15 when using BCD the numbers above nine are not used.

Decimal	Binary Coded Decimal
0	0000 0000
1	0000 0001
2	0000 0010
3	0000 0011
4	0000 0100
5	0000 0101
6	0000 0110
7	0000 0111
8	0000 1000
9	0000 1001
10	0001 0000

Bit
This stands for BInary digiT. It is the base unit of data consisting of a 0 or a 1.

Bit Rate
The speed at which bits of data can be sent.

Block
A fixed amount of data. This term is often used when referring to a section of data which is stored on a disk or magnetic tape.

Bomb Out
This phrase refers to a program failure. It is often reserved for occasions when the program fails disasterously.

Boolean Algebra
This is a form of algebra named after the nineteenth-century English mathematician George Boole. It uses an algebraic form of notation to represent logical operations. The Boolean operators normally found within a computer language are AND, OR and NOT.

Boot
See Bootstrap.

Bootstrap
This refers to the process of initially loading in a system program into a computer and running it to enable the computer to operate. The name is derived from the idea of the computer pulling itself up by its own bootstraps.

Branch
A change from the straightforward incremental order of executing instructions. A branch may be conditional upon various parameters being fulfilled or it may be unconditional.

Branch Instruction
An instruction which causes the program execution to branch to another point within the program.

Bubble Memory
See Magnetic Bubble Memory.

Buffer
A section of memory used as a temporary holding area when transferring data from one place to another.

Bug
An error in a program.

Bus

This is a group of wires, normally eight or sixteen, used to transfer data from place to place within a system. There are normally several devices attached to the bus. Only one is allowed to transmit data onto it at any one time, and usually only one will be enabled so that it can listen. Therefore one set of wires can be used to link several devices.

Bus Driver

An electronic circuit used to transmit signals onto a data bus.

Byte

This is a unit of information consisting of a set number of bits. There are usually 8 bits in a byte although sometimes there may be 16 or 32.

C

C
A medium-level language designed for general-purpose applications. Although initially written for use only on one system it is now being used on many types of machine.

Cambridge Ring
A standard for a local area network where all the stations are connected in a ring configuration. The interface device to each station incorporates a synchronous shift register. When one station requires to transmit it looks for an empty "slot" when no other station is transmitting and then proceeds to transmit its data packet which includes both source and destination addresses. When not transmitting, stations will monitor the ring for packets of information bearing their address as destination.

Card
A printed circuit board with its components. *See also* punched card.

Card Punch
A unit for putting information onto punched cards. The information is in the form of small holes punched into the card.

Card Reader
A unit for reading the information from punched cards.

Carriage Return
An action which causes the next character which is to be printed or displayed to appear in the left-hand margin. Carriage return may also refer to the code which causes a carriage return to take place, i.e., ASCII character 13 (decimal) or 0D (hexadecimal).

Carry
The name given to the digit transferred to the next position higher up when two digits added together exceed the base.

Catalog(ue)
A directory of the files stored on a disk.

Cathode Ray Tube
A thermionic tube or valve used for displaying visual images. They are used in televisions and also in computer monitors and VDUs.

Cell
An element of storage which can store one bit.

Central Processing Unit
That area of a computer in which the actual computation and manipulation of the data takes place.

Chain
To organise a program so that when it has completed execution it runs another program. Programs may be chained if a large program has to be split into sections in order that it may not overflow the available memory.

Character
Any letter, digit, punctuation mark or symbol used to display information.

Character Set
The set of letters, digits, punctuation marks and symbols recognised within a particular computer.

Check Sum
The result of a summation of a block of data which is often used when transmitting or storing data. The check sum will be generated before and after the process and both results compared to indicate whether an error has occurred.

Chip
Another name for an integrated circuit.

Clear
To remove the contents of one or more registers or memory locations i.e., set the contents to zero or some other pre-determined value.

Clock
A clock is the timing source used to synchronise operations within a computer, electronic circuit or system.

COBOL
This stands for COmmon Business Orientated Language. It is the computer language used for most business and commercial applications.

Code
The statements, either in compiled or text form, which make a program.

Cold Start
A cold start or cold boot is performed when a computer is powered on, or restarted as if from power-on. This is accomplished by loading in and running the operating system for the computer.

Command
An instruction to the computer normally entered directly from a keyboard in order to instruct it to perform a task.

Comment
A statement included within a program which is ignored by the assembler, compiler or interpreter and does not affect the running of a program. It serves only to explain or remind the programmer about the function of a particular section of the program.

Compiler

A program which converts a text program into machine language ready for execution by the computer. The overall program is compiled before execution and the text or source code and the compiled or object code are normally stored on disk before execution.

Complement

A process in which each digit of a number is subtracted from one less than the base. If one is added to the result the true complement is formed otherwise omitting this the nine's complement is formed in a decimal system or one's complement in a binary system. For example, the nine's complement of 304 is 695 and one's complement of 1010 is 0101. The complement of a number is used in computers when subtracting numbers as it enables subtraction to be performed by adding numbers together. This method is far easier to implement than any other.

Computer

A machine which can process data entered into it according to a set of instructions given to it so that an output is obtained.

Computer Language

The defined instruction set which can be used to program a computer in order to enable it to perform various tasks. These languages may be at a low level where the programmer enters instruction in machine code, or in a form similar to machine code, or at a high level which is more easily understood by the programmer but requires converting into machine code by a compiler or interpreter.

Concatenate

To join together end to end. This term is often used in conjunction with joining strings together where the second string is joined to the end of the first to form one long string.

Conditional Statement

A statement of which the outcome is dependent upon certain conditions being fulfilled. One example of this is the IF statement used in many languages.

Console

The unit with which a computer operator communicates with the computer. It may incorporate a keyboard or switches and it displays information from the computer

Constant

A data item which remains unchanged during a program. Normally a constant will be assigned its value at the beginning of a program e.g., PI = 3·1416.

Contention

A contention is said to occur when two units are trying to access the same device simultaneously. This type of problem is often encountered with local area networks when two computers attempt to send data onto the network at the same time. Provision has to be made to overcome this problem.

Control Character

A non-printable character used to issue controlling commands often to peripheral devices. These control characters are accessed from the keyboard by depressing the CONTROL key at the same time as typing the required character. *See* Appendices 1 and 2 for a list of ASCII control characters and codes.

Conversion Error

Owing to the fact that a computer can only work to a limited number of figures small errors occur. This type of error is known as a conversion error.

CORAL

This is a high-level language which is used extensively for real-time applications.

Core

A term which was originally used to refer to the magnetic ferrite core memory which was found within computers. Often the term is still used to refer to a computer's memory.

CP/M

This stands for Control Program for Microcomputers and it is an operating system which can be run on many microcomputers. CP/M is a trade mark of Digital Research Inc.

CPS

Characters Per Second. This refers to the rate of sending data. CPS used to stand for cycles per second, however, the unit Hertz (abbreviated to Hz) is now used as the unit of frequency.

CPU

See Central Processing Unit.

Crash

A computer crash is a situation where the computer has stopped working and has to be manually restarted, or it has to be repaired.

CRT

See Cathode Ray Tube.

Current Loop

A system used for transmitting serial data to and from a peripheral device such as a printer or teletype. It involves switching on and off a current source which normally provides 20 mA.

Cursor

A marker displayed on a screen to indicate where the next typed character will appear.

Cycle Stealing

A technique of suspending the operation of a processor whilst slow peripherals respond.

Cycle Time
The time taken for the computer processor to complete a given operation.

D

DAC
See D/A Converter.

D/A Converter
An electronic circuit, often a single integrated circuit, for converting digital information to an analogue signal.

Daisy Wheel Printer
This type of printer uses a wheel very similar to the flower of a daisy i.e., it has a central core with many radial spokes attached. At the end of each spoke is a raised letter which, when the daisy wheel is correctly orientated and the letter then impacted onto an inked ribbon, prints the corresponding letter onto the paper.

Data
Data is information which is entered into a computer and then subsequently manipulated by a program.

Data Base
A data file organised in a fashion which the data from it can be processed by a computer often by several different programs.

Data Base Management System
This is a type of computer program used for collecting, storing, manipulating and displaying information in a useable form from a data base.

Data Channel
A communications line over which data may be transmitted usually in both directions.

Data Link

Some form of link for transferring data from one place to another. Often a telephone line is used with a modem at either end of the link.

Debug

To remove the errors or bugs from a program.

Debugger

A program for indicating syntax errors within a program.

Declaration

A statement which usually occurs at the beginning of a program or routine which defines the size, type or other information about the variables used.

Decrement

To reduce in steps, usually by one.

Dedicated

This refers to equipment which is used for one purpose or by one computer only.

Default

In a computer system where a value has to be assigned and none is specified by the program or by the programmer then the computer will often choose the value, usually zero or other convenient value. In this case it is said to default to a certain value.

Delimiter

A character or set of characters used within a language or program to identify the start or finish of a particular section. For example, " within a PRINT statement in BASIC indicates the start and finish of a section of text and is therefore a delimiter.

Destructive Read

This refers to the method of reading data in some memories

17

e.g., ferrite core memories where the data is destroyed in the memory when it is accessed. In order to preserve the data in the memory it has to be re-written into it.

Digit
A numeric character i.e., in decimal one of the characters in the range 0 to 9.

Digital
Describes a system which represents values in the form of numbers. In electronic systems digital numbers are represented in a binary format.

Digital Computer
A computer which employs digital methods.

Digitise
To convert to a digital form.

DIP
See Dual In-line Package.

Direct Addressing
A mode of addressing memory locations in which the address does not require any processing by the CPU.

Direct Memory Access
A mechanism for directly accessing the memory of a computer with minimal CPU intervention and for transferring large amounts of data at high speed to a peripheral device. As the CPU is only involved in the set-up and has no involvement in the transfer itself the speed of operation is increased.

Directory
A catalogue or list of the files stored on a disk.

Disassembler
A program which converts a program from machine code into

assembly language i.e., the reverse of an assembler.

Disc or Disk
A storage medium which is made up from a flat circular plate on which the surface is covered with a magnetic material. Data can then be recorded onto this surface and read from it as it is rotated.

Disk Controller
A hardware circuit which controls the data passing between a computer and its associated disk drive.

Disk Drive
The unit consisting of electronic circuits, motors, heads, etc., which enables data to be written onto and read from disks.

Diskette
A term used to refer to the smaller floppy disks, normally those which are 5¼ inches or smaller.

Disk Head
The magnetic head performs the actual writing and reading of data to and from the disk surface.

Disk Operating System
A set of software or commands which enables the computer to write data to and read data from a disk system.

DMA
See Direct Memory Access.

DOS
See Disk Operating System.

Dot Matrix Printer
A type of printer which prints by impacting a matrix of print wires onto an inked ribbon to make up the required shape for a character.

Down

A computer or other piece of equipment is said to be down if it is not functioning and is awaiting repair.

Dual In-line Package

A standard configuration for integrated circuit casings consisting of the integrated circuit package with two rows of pins, one each side with each pin spaced 0·1 inch away from the next.

Dump

To transfer the complete contents of a section of memory or a file to another location.

Duplex

This refers to a system which permits data to be transmitted along a data channel in both directions simultaneously.

Dynamic RAM

A type of random access memory requiring a refresh pulse to be applied to it every few milliseconds in order to maintain the data within the memory. The advantage of this type of memory is that as the data is stored as the charge on a capacitor it enables the memory to be very dense and to have a low power consumption.

E

EBCDIC
See Extended Binary Coded Decimal Interchange Code.

Echo
This is a term used to describe a means of ensuring that data
has been correctly received where the unit receiving the data
sends back or echoes the data to the transmitter where it can
be checked.

EDP
See Electronic Data Processing.

Edit
To modify or change a work file or piece of text.

Editor
The program which controls the editing of a text file or text
program.

Electronic Data Processing
A term used to refer to the processing of data by a computer.

Emulate
The process of making one computer or unit look like another so that the software for the second may be used by the
first. This may be accomplished by the use of either software
or hardware.

Enabled
A unit is said to be enabled when it has been put into a state
which it will operate.

EPROM
Eraseable Programmable Read Only Memory. A type of

PROM which can be erased usually by exposing it to ultra-violet light. There are small opaque windows in the top of the integrated circuit packages to enable the light to reach the circuit itself. When erased the EPROM may be re-programmed and used again.

Error Message
A message produced by a computer to indicate a program error. Error messages usually indicate the nature and location of the error.

Escape
A character found on many keyboards corresponding to ASCII decimal value 27 or hexadecimal value 1B. It is often used to set the keyboard to a different mode or to indicate that the following character belongs to a different character set.

Ethernet
A standard for a local area network. If a station requires to transmit data it listens on the network until a gap is detected when no data is being transmitted and it then sends its data with a destination address. If two stations happen to transmit at the same time they detect the contention and back off for a random amount of time.

Exclusive OR
A logical operation from which a logical 1 or true is obtained if either but not both of the input digits is logical 1 or true, otherwise the output obtained is a logical 0 or false.

Exclusive OR Gate
An electronic circuit which provides an exclusive OR function.

Execute
To run a program.

Executive
A program which is used to manage, supervise or monitor the running of a computer.

Exponent
The number of times a variable or expression is multiplied by itself i.e., the power to which it is raised.

Expression
A mathematical or logical statement which has been put into a form which can be accepted by a computer.

Extended Binary Coded Decimal Interchange Code
The code which is used for data communication within most IBM computers.

F

Field
An individual section of data within a record. For example, if a record were made up from a day, month and year then day, month and year individually would constitute a field.

FIFO
This stands for First In First Out. It refers to a type of register in which the first data entered will be the first out.

File
A particular set of data, a program etc., stored on a medium such as a tape or disk.

File Server
A term used in the context of local area networks which refers to the unit that handles the disk input and output requests from users on the network. Normally there will be one central disk drive or set of drives on a network and all the co-ordination of data to and from the drives and onto the network is handled by the file server.

Firmware
Data or programs stored within a read only memory.

Fixed Point Arithmetic
A type of notation where arithmetic calculations are performed without consideration for the decimal point.

Flag
A single bit of information held within memory to indicate that a particular event has happened.

Floating Point Arithmetic
A method of holding and manipulating numbers within a

computer where the number is stored as two parts: the significant digits; and the exponent.

Floppy Disk
A disk made of flexible plastic surfaced with a magnetic medium. It is normally enclosed in a special card jacket for protection, but small areas are exposed to enable the disk heads to have access and to enable it to be rotated.

Flowchart
A diagram which is drawn to represent the order of events within a program. When drawing flowcharts it is usual to use a conventional set of symbols to represent each type of event.

Format
To format or initialise a disk is to set it up ready to receive data. This is done by writing information onto it which divides its surface into tracks and sectors. It can also refer to a computer language statement which specifies the way in which printed or displayed data is set out.

Forth
A high-level structured language initially envisaged for use within control systems but now often used on microcomputers as a general-purpose language.

Fortran
A high-level computer language used mainly for scientific applications. Its name is derived from the two words FORmula TRANslation.

Full Duplex
This refers to a data channel or unit which allows data transmission in both directions simultaneously.

Function

Within a computer language a function is a routine whose name takes the value for the given parameters, e.g., SIN(X) etc.

G

Gate

A digital electronic circuit for which the logical output is dependent upon certain input states. The logical functions, AND, OR, NAND and NOR are performed by these gates.

GIGO

This stands for Garbage In Garbage Out. It refers to the fact that the output from a computer will only be as accurate as the data which has been entered.

Global Variable

A variable which can be accessed by all parts of a computer program.

GPIB

General Purpose Interface Bus. *See* IEEE 488 bus.

Graphics

The display of pictures or diagrams onto a computer monitor or VDU screen.

H

Half Duplex
This refers to a data channel or unit which can send data in both directions but not simultaneously.

Handshaking
A communications protocol where data transmitting and receiving units pass signals indicating whether further data can be transmitted or accepted. This is particularly useful where data can be transmitted faster that it can be absorbed by the terminal device. The data flow can then be interrupted when the terminal is not ready for data and restarted when it is again ready.

Hard Copy
A copy of data from a computer in a readable form which can be removed from the computer environment e.g., a printout from a printer.

Hard Disk
A non-flexible disk. Hard disks are able to store more data than a floppy disk but they are still more expensive, and therefore they tend to be used on larger computer installations.

Hardware
This refers to the tangible electronic (and mechanical) devices which constitute a system.

Head
This usually refers to the electromagnetic head which performs the actual reading and writing of the data from and to the surface of the disk.

Head Crash
A head crash occurs on a hard disk system when the head, which normally "flies" a few microinches above the surface of the disk, hits the surface causing corruption of the data and damage to the disk.

Heuristic
Describes a method of finding solutions to problems by trial and error using successive attempts and modifications to reach the final solution.

Hex
A shortened name for hexadecimal.

Hexadecimal
A numbering system which uses the base 16 and employs sixteen digits which are represented by 0 to 9 then A to F. Each hexadecimal digit can be represented by four binary ones.

Hexadecimal	Decimal	Binary
0	0	0000
1	1	0001
2	2	0010
3	3	0011
4	4	0100
5	5	0101
6	6	0110
7	7	0111
8	8	1000
9	9	1001
A	10	1010
B	11	1011
C	12	1100
D	13	1101
E	14	1110
F	15	1111

High-level Language
A computer language in which instructions are written in a form easily understood by users. Typically one high-level language statement will correspond to several machine code ones. Examples of high-level languages are BASIC, Pascal, Fortran, etc.

Highway
A data bus.

Housekeeping
A function performed periodically within a computer to remove unwanted data from memory and generally set the computer so that it is able to handle further programs efficiently.

I

Identifier
A label consisting of letters and numbers which is used to identify something, e.g. variable, constant, file, etc.

IEEE 488 Bus
A bus system for transferring data between a controller and up to fourteen other remote stations. The system sends data in a bit parallel byte serial form and includes a very comprehensive handshaking system. Originally envisaged as a bus system for controlling test instruments and collecting data from them it is now used for many other purposes including sending data from a computer to a printer. The name is derived from the fact that the bus is defined in standard number 488 issued by the Institute of Electrical and Electronics Engineers in the USA.

Implicit Addressing
A method of addressing memory locations in which the address is not specifically stated but implicitly forms part of the instruction. It is normally used in conjunction with instructions which operate only on registers which can be specified as part of the instruction.

Increment
To increase a variable or other parameter, usually by one.

Index Addressing
A method of addressing memory locations in which the address of the required data is found using an index register which is incremented or decremented by one each time it is accessed. This type of addressing is normally used to successively access the contents of a table.

Indirect Addressing

A method of addressing memory locations in which the data in the address stated gives the location where the required data is situated. This type of addressing is particularly useful when writing sub-routines which by their very nature need to be kept general.

Initialise

To set the variables used in a program or sub-routine to a known starting state at the beginning of computation. It can also mean to format a disk.

Ink Jet Printer

A form of printer which prints by controlling a jet or set of jets of ink so that the required shapes are marked onto paper. One of the main advantages of this type of printer is the low levels of acoustic noise which are emitted, making it very suitable for many office applications.

Input

To enter data into a computer.

Instruction Register

The name given to the register which holds the instruction which is currently being executed.

Instruction Set

The full list of commands which the computer or other unit will comprehend and obey.

Integer

A whole number; a number without a fractional part.

Integer Arithmetic

Arithmetic which can only handle integers i.e., no fractional parts to numbers can be handled.

Interactive

Describes a method of operation where there is two-way communication or interaction between the computer and user.

Interface
This term refers to the circuitry connecting one set of circuits to another. Similarly it can also refer to the software which links one section of software to another.

Interpreter
This is software which converts a program written in a high-level language to machine code, converting and implementing it on an instruction by instruction basis. Compare with a compiler.

Interrupt
A signal to a processor indicating that it should temporarily stop execution of the current task to perform a more urgent one.

Interrupt Priority
In processors which possess several interrupt lines an order of priority for dealing with the interrupt has to be created. This order is known as the interrupt priority.

I/O
This stands for Input/Output. For example, an I/O port is capable of handling both inputs and outputs.

Iteration
A process whereby an instruction or set of instructions is repeatedly executed.

J

JCL
See Job Control Language.

Job
A program or set of programs presented to a computer complete with data for execution. This term is normally used where there are large computers using batch processing techniques.

Job Control Language
The language used on a computer to control the running of jobs.

Jump
See Branch.

Justify
To modify the left-hand, right-hand, or both margins so that the margins form a regular vertical line.

K

Karnaugh Map
A graphical plot of a truth table.

Keyboard
A unit for converting characters into an electrical form by using the manual depressions of marked keys. It is normally very similar in layout to a typewriter keyboard.

Key In
To type data or programs into a computer.

Kilo
A prefix meaning one thousand, e.g., one kilobyte is one thousand bytes.

L

Label
A name given to a set of characters used to define an area of memory or a point within a program.

LAN
See Local Area Network.

Large-scale Integration
The scale of integration required to put a very large number of components onto a single integrated circuit. For example, large-scale integration is required to manufacture microprocessors.

Latch
A latch is an electronic circuit for holding data. The data presented at the input of a latch will only be transferred and subsequently held at the output when an enable pulse is applied to the circuit. The data will be held unchanged at the output until the next enable pulse is applied and the new data transferred.

Library
A set of commonly-used routines, programs, etc. stored on tape or disk for general use. It is very common for manufacturers to supply libraries with computer equipment.

LIFO
This stands for Last In First Out. Data in a stack is handled in this fashion where the last data in will be the first out.

Light Pen
A hand-held photosensitive module in the shape of a pen which can be used with a monitor or VDU screen to draw shapes on the screen or by holding it to certain preset areas

on the screen it can tell the computer to perform a particular function.

Linker
This is a program which links the object code of separately written parts of a program.

Literal
This is a term which refers to a character which stands for itself only, i.e., not a variable name, etc.

Local Area Network
This is a method of linking several computers, often microcomputers so that they are able to communicate with each other and usually there is also a central storage unit consisting of one or more disk drives.

Logo
A programming language developed for educational purposes.

Loop
A loop consists of a set of instructions which the computer executes repeatedly. At the end of the loop there is an instruction which diverts to the beginning of the loop once again. Either at the beginning or at the end of the loop there is a conditional statement which enables the computer to jump out of the loop when certain conditions are fulfilled.

Low-level Language
Any programming language in which the instructions are written in a similar form to the machine code and in which typically one low-level language instruction will correspond to one machine code instruction. One example of this is assembly language.

LSB
Least Significant Bit. A term used to describe the bit within a byte of data having the least significant or smallest value.

LSI

See Large-scale Integration.

M

Machine Code
The instructions or code which are executed directly by the processor. Instructions in machine code can be comprehended by the processor with no alteration i.e., the language of the processor.

Machine Language
See Machine Code.

Macro
A sequence of assembly language instructions which can be inserted into the object code of a program wherever the assembler finds the name for that particular macro.

Macro Assembler
An assembler which has the capabilities of handling macros.

Macro Instruction
An assembly language instruction which calls a macro.

Magnetic Bubble Memory
This is a form of memory based upon the concept of magnetic "bubbles" or cylinders which form in a particular type of crystal. These bubbles can be manipulated in such a form that they can be used to store data. Although they are not at present in widespread use it is possible that future systems may employ them quite extensively.

Matrix
A matrix is an array having two or more dimensions. They are widely used when dealing with tabular information because matrices form a very convenient method of handling this type of data. An example of a two-dimensional matrix would be a table consisting of rows and columns.

Mega

A prefix indicating one million, e.g. one megabyte is one million bytes.

Memory

That portion of the computer hardware where data, programs, variables, etc. are stored.

Memory Map

A diagram showing the areas of memory used or reserved for various functions, programs, etc. within the computer.

Memory Mapped I/O

A method used for transferring data to and from peripherals where a memory location is used as an input/output port.

Menu

A selection of choices given by a computer program to enable a user to select the required option.

Microcomputer

A computer based on a microprocessor.

Microprocessor

A computer processor contained on a single integrated circuit. Integrated circuits such as the Z80, 6502, 8080 and 6800 are all examples of microprocessors.

Minicomputer

A computer more powerful than a microcomputer, being able to execute instructions more quickly, access more memory and normally able to handle larger words. It is however, smaller than a main frame computer. A precise definition of a minicomputer is not possible because the boundaries which limit micro, mini and main frame computers are continually changing as new and better technology are introduced.

Mnemonic

A name chosen to represent an item in order to aid the user's memory.

Modem

This stands for MOdulator DEModulator. It is a device which converts computer data to a form that can be transmitted onto and also received from a telephone line.

Monitor

A program which manages the system operation and controls the operation of programs within the computer. It can also refer to a display which can only be used for viewing information and does not include a keyboard.

MOS

This stands for Metal-Oxide-Silicon and is a form of technology used for fabricating field effect transistors and their derivative integrated circuits. Various extensions of this technology have been introduced to enhance the performance of various integrated circuits by reducing power consumption and increasing speed. CMOS, NMOS, CHMOS represent a few of these enhancements.

MP/M

This stands for Multiprogramming control Program for Microcomputers. It is an operating system which can be used on many microcomputers. MP/M is a trade mark of Digital Research Inc.

MSB

Most Significant Bit. A term used to describe the bit within a byte of data having the highest value or most significance.

Multiplex

To send several signals along the same line. This may be achieved in several ways; by using different frequencies, different time slots, etc.

N

NAND Gate
An electronic circuit which provides a NOT AND function, i.e. its output is a logical 0 if both of its inputs are a logical 1, otherwise the output is a logical 1.

Nest
This refers to a program construction where there is a loop within a loop, subroutine called within a subroutine, etc. Very often a computer will place limits on levels of nesting especially of subroutines, beyond this limit an error will be indicated.

Network
See Local Area Network.

Nibble
Half a byte. It is normally 4 bits long.

Non-destructive Read
This refers to the reading mechanism within a memory where after the data has been read it still remains intact.

Non-volatile
This refers to a type of memory in which the data is retained even when the power is removed.

NOR
A logical function from which a logical 0 or false is obtained if either or both inputs are logical 1 or true, otherwise the output is 1. NOR is a contraction of NOT OR.

NOR Gate
An electronic circuit which provides a NOR function.

NOT
A logical function in which the result is the inverse of the input.

Numerical Analysis
The application of methods of finding numerical solutions to problems with the associated errors in the results.

Numerical Control
A method of controlling machines, especially machine tools e.g., lathes, etc. by the use of encoded data. This can be achieved in its simplest form by the use of a prepared paper tape or by more advanced methods using full computer control.

Nybble
See Nibble.

O

Object Code
The code which is in a form which can be executed by a machine, i.e,. a program in its compiled or assembled form.

Octal
A numbering system using the base eight having digits in the range 0 to 7. As three binary digits are able to represent an octal number it is often used as a convenient way of representing binary numbers.

Octal	Decimal	Binary
0	0	000 000
1	1	000 001
2	2	000 010
3	3	000 011
4	4	000 100
5	5	000 101
6	6	000 110
7	7	000 111
10	8	001 000
11	9	001 001
12	10	001 010

Off-line
A unit is said to be off-line when it is in a mode in which it is not able to communicate with its associated computer.

On-line
A unit is said to be on-line when it is in a mode in which it is able to communicate with its associated computer.

Operating System
The set of software which co-ordinates the computer enabling programs to be executed in a logical and efficient manner.

OR

A logical function from which a logical 1 or true is obtained if either or both of the inputs are a logical 1 or true, otherwise the result is a logical 0 or false.

OR Gate

An electronic circuit which provides an OR function.

Overflow

The result of an operation, usually a mathematical one, which is too large for the computer to store. An error message usually results.

Overhead

This refers to any quantity such as time, memory, etc. which the computer uses for system operation and not directly for execution of a program.

Overlay

To re-use parts of a computer's memory for storing sections of a program only when they are required. If a program is too large to be stored in memory all at the same time then only those parts of the program essential to the overall running of the program are held in memory all the time and other sections of the program are brought into memory from an external device such as a disk when they are required and cleared when they are no longer needed.

P

Pack
To insert more than one data item into a word. Data can be packed in order to save storage space, but doing this utilises more computer time as a penalty.

Paper Tape
This is a storage medium consisting of a tape of paper normally one inch or twenty-five millimetres wide into which holes are punched to encode data. This can later be read back. Although still quite widely used, this method of data storage is slow in operation and the tapes are bulky for the amount of data stored.

Parallel Interface
An interface over which several bits, usually one byte of data at a time is transmitted, each bit requiring one wire. After the information has been accepted the data transmitter will send a new set of data.

Parallel Printer
A printer which receives its data over a parallel interface.

Parameter
A constant, variable or other quantity passed into or out of a subroutine or function.

Parity
The parity of a byte of data is said to be even if the total number of ones is even, and conversely, the parity is odd if the number of ones is odd.

Parity Bit
The eighth bit within a byte of data is often used as a parity bit to make up the overall parity of the byte to an even or odd

parity. The parity of data received by a system can be checked to detect any data errors.

Pascal
A high-level computer programming language named after the French mathematician. It uses rigid structuring techniques and was designed initially to teach good programming methods.

Pass
A single execution of a loop or section of a program. It is also often used in connection with the action of a compiler or assembler as sometimes more than one pass will be required to complete compilation or assembly.

Password
A word or group of words entered into a computer so that access can be gained to the computer or to a particular set of programs.

P-Code
The compiled form of a Pascal program. When a Pascal program is compiled it does not give a directly machine executable form of code but one which has to be executed on an interpreter basis. Although this does make the program run more slowly than one in machine code it does have the advantage that the p-code can be transferred between different types of machine.

Peripheral
A unit connected to a computer to enable it to perform extra functions. They are usually input, output or storage devices such as a keyboard, printer or disk drive.

Personal Computer
A desk-top computer intended for personal use. It does not have multi-user access via terminals.

Pilot
A high-level language designed for educational purposes. Pilot stands for Programmed Inquiry, Learning Or Teaching.

PL/1
This stands for Programming Language 1 and it is a high-level stuctured language.

PL/M
This is a high-level language developed from PL/1 but designed and used primarily for developing software for microprocessor-based systems.

Pointer
An address indicating where a particular piece of information may be found. Addresses are only referred to as pointers when they indicate or point to where a piece of data may be found or where a data structure begins or ends. One example of a pointer is the stack pointer which indicates the address of the last piece of data added to the stack.

Polish Notation
An algebraic notation in which variables are placed in front of their operators.

Poll
A process of interrogating several devices in turn to enquire if they require attention. For example, devices can be polled if a shared interrupt line is activated to ascertain which device requested the interrupt.

Pop
A term used in machine language programming to show that a byte of data has been removed from the stack.

Port
A port is a point of entry or exit for data from a system. It often gives access onto the bus system within a computer.

Primitive
This refers to the lowest levels of instruction for a system i.e., low-level language instructions and machine code.

Printer
A unit for transferring data from a computer onto paper in a permanent form.

Print Server
A term used in the context of local area networks which refers to the unit which handles the print requests from users on the network. When using a network it is often useful to have a central printer which handles the printing requirements for the whole network. The print server receives and controls the data from network to be printed.

Problem Orientated Language
A language designed for solving problems in a particular field. Two examples of problem orientated languages are Fortran which is orientated towards solving scientific problems and Cobol which is used for business applications.

Procedure
A subroutine.

Processor
The circuitry within a computer in which the computation is performed. It is the processor which executes the data and controls the rest of the hardware.

Program
A set of instructions written in a computer language to enable the computer to fulfil a specific function.

Program Counter
The register within the computer processor in which the address of the next instruction to be performed is held.

Programmable Read Only Memory
A type of ROM which is manufactured with no data programmed into it. The data is entered by the user via a PROM programmer.

Programmer
A person who writes computer programs.

PROM
See Programmable Read Only Memory.

Pseudo Instruction
An instruction arranged in a symbolic form to aid in the compilation or assembly of a program.

Pseudo Random Number
A number generated as part of a sequence of numbers derived from a mathematical calculation to simulate a random number sequence. Pseudo random number sequences are used in computers as they are easy to generate and quite adequate for most purposes.

Pull
See Pop.

Punched Card
A storage medium consisting of a paper card into which small rectangular holes are punched to encode data. The card is divided into twelve rows and eighty columns with each column corresponding to a byte of data.

Push
A term used in machine language programming to show that a byte of data has been added to the stack.

Q

Queue
To line tasks up in order so that a device may execute them
sequentially, e.g. several programs may be queued so that a
computer may execute them as it has time.

Quotient
The result of dividing one number by another ignoring the
remainder which may be produced.

R

RAM
See Random Access Memory.

Radio Frequency Interference
This is interference generated by electrical or electronic equipment (in this case computers and their peripherals) which interferes with the reception on nearby radios and televisions.

Radix
See Base.

Random Access Memory
This is a type of memory used to store data temporarily within a computer. Data can be written onto it and also read from it. Programs, variables, pointers, etc. are stored within this memory which is effectively the work area.

Read Only Memory
This is a type of memory which is programmed during manufacture and can only be used to read the stored data. ROMs are normally used to store data or programs which have to be held intact whilst the equipment is switched off, and ones which are frequently required. One example of this is the language ROM within a microcomputer.

Real
This refers to a number which has both integer and fractional parts.

Real-Time
This expression is used to refer to a system which is able to respond to circumstances as they happen. For example, a computer acting as a controller for a system operates in real-

time because it has to respond to events as they occur. Alternatively, a program analysing data taken from a series of experiments would not operate in real-time.

Record
A group of related data elements stored as a group. For example, date is a record consisting of day, month and year.

Refresh
A refresh pulse is a pulse which is applied every few milliseconds to a dynamic memory to restore the charge held in the memory cells and thus retain the data.

Register
A special temporary storage location attached to a processor to enable it to perform its various functions. Processors will have several registers: accumulator; index register; etc.

Relational Operator
A sign which relates a value, variable or expression to another e.g., =, <, >, <> or # (not equal to), <= (less than or equal to), etc.

Relative Addressing
A method of addressing memory locations in which the computer accesses information a stated number of locations away from the present one.

Resident
This describes a program or routine which is always located in the computer memory.

Reverse Polish Notation
An algebraic notation in which variables are followed by their operators.

RFI
see Radio Frequency Interference.

ROM
See Read Only Memory.

Rotate
A type of machine code instruction in which the bits of data in a register are moved a certain number of places to the left or right. Any bits which come out of one end of the register enter the other end.

Rounding Error
An error in the accuracy of numbers introduced by rounding a number off. The error is normally too small to become apparent but there may be occasions when it does become significant and it should be taken into account.

Routine
A subroutine.

RS232
A very widely-used standard for serial data transmission. It is extensively employed for applications such as sending data to a printer or VDU from a computer.

Run
To execute or perform a program.

Run-Time
Something which occurs during the running of a program is described as a run-time event. For example, an error which occurs during the running of a program is said to be a run-time error.

S

Scientific Notation
A notation for representing numbers where the number is expressed as its significant numbers between ·1000 and ·9999 and a decimal multiplier or exponent. For example, 379·3 would be represented as ·3793 × 10^3 or often when printed by a computer ·3793 E3 as computer printers are usually unable to print superscripts.

Scroll
To change the information being displayed on a screen by adding new information to the bottom and moving all the remaining information up, and losing the top line. This can of course be performed in the reverse direction.

Sector
This is a fixed portion of track on a magnetic disk containing a fixed amount of data. Disks are split up into tracks and sectors for the purposes of addressing the correct part of the disk.

Segment
A section of a program which has been split into parts.

Serial Interface
An interface over which data is transmitted or received in a sequential manner one bit after another.

Serial Printer
A printer which accepts data over a serial interface.

Shift
A machine code instruction which moves data in a register to the left or right.

Sign Bit

The bit in a binary number used to indicate the sign of the number. Negative binary numbers are often represented by the complement of the number and hence the left-hand bit indicates a positive number if it is zero and a negative number if it is one.

Software

The programs or code within a computer, stored on disk, tape, etc. or held within some other unit.

Sort

A routine for re-arranging a set of information in a random sequence into the required logical order. There are several different methods of sorting, each possessing its own merits and used in particular applications.

Source Code

The code from which the object code is derived. It is the program written in a computer language before compilation or assembly.

Spool

This stands for Simultaneous Peripheral Output On Line. It refers to a method in which a computer is able to make efficient use of its hardware for computation whilst still attending to its input and output functions which are by their nature slow.

Stack

An area of memory used for the temporary storage of data, e.g. the return addresses of subroutines and so forth. There are special operations associated with the operation of a stack – *see* Pop and Push.

Stack Pointer

A pointer which stores the location of the last item added to the stack.

Stand Alone
This term refers to a system which can operate on its own without a requirement for any further equipment.

Start Bit
The first element of a byte of data sent along an asynchronous data channel to indicate the start of the byte.

Statement
An instruction in a computer language.

Status Register
A register within a computer which holds bits of information each of which give information about the condition of the processor.

Status Word
A word of information indicating information about the condition of the processor or some other unit.

Stop Bit
The last element of a byte of data sent along an asynchronous data channel to indicate the end of the byte of data.

String
A line or set of characters. A string is similar to a one-dimensional array with character elements.

Structured Programming
A logical method of writing computer programs in a way that they are easy to understand and modify. The first stage in programming consists of defining the problem and then breaking it down into smaller tasks. These in turn may be broken down still further. Each task is then represented by a subroutine or procedure, which can call subroutines that represent the subtasks. Thus the program is written in a logical straightforward manner.

Structured Language
A computer language designed to enable users to use structured programming techniques.

Subroutine
A set of instructions which performs a specific task which is required as part of a program. The subroutine will have defined entry and exit points so that it can be used by several different parts of the program as required.

Successive Approximation
This is a method of solving complicated equations by initially estimating a result, calculating the equation and then entering a further value closer to the solution. The process is repeated until a solution is found giving a sufficiently small error. The method of successive approximation is a particularly useful one when used with computers because they are able to perform iterative processes like this very fast.

Synchronous
A system is referred to as synchronous if a clock is required to maintain synchronism between the various elements within the system.

Syntax
The rules governing the way in which the statements in a computer language must be written.

System
A set of constituents which operate together as a complete unit to enable tasks to be performed. For example, a computer system may consist of a computer with disk drive, monitor and printer so that programs may be written, stored, executed and the results printed out.

T

Tape Drive
A unit for writing data onto magnetic tape. This term normally refers to the large units used on main frame computers.

Tape Punch
A mechanical punch for punching holes into paper tape to encode data.

Tape Streamer
A unit used for writing data onto magnetic tape in a cassette and retrieving data from it. Tape streamers are often used in conjunction with smaller computer systems to provide a backup for a hard disk drive in case of data corruptions.

Teleprinter
An electromechanical printer with a keyboard bearing a resemblance to a typewriter and used for sending and receiving data to and from a computer, often over a data link. They often have a paper tape reader and punch as an integral part of the unit.

Teletypewriter
See Teleprinter.

Terminal
A unit used for entering and receiving data from a computer. Terminals are often remote from the computer and connected to it via a data channel.

Text
Information or programs presented in a readable form.

Text Editor
See Editor.

Thermal Printer
A type of printer which prints by using a set of localised heat points to put the required marks onto special heat-sensitive paper.

Throughput
This refers to the amount of work which can be handled by a given computer or other unit.

Time Sharing
This is a system of operation enabling several users each with their own terminal to run programs concurrently on one computer. The term derives its name from the fact that the processor shares its time between different users.

Top Down Programming
See Structured Programming.

Track
A band or circle on a magnetic disk a fixed distance from the centre where data is written. Each disk will have many tracks and these are divided in turn into sectors.

Truncate
To remove some of the least significant figures of a number without rounding off the number.

Truth Table
A tabulation of Boolean relationships between variables, usually representing true as 1 and false as 0.

TTL
This stands for Transistor Transistor Logic. It is a family of logical integrated circuits which are very widely used.

TTY

Teletypewriter.

Turnkey

This refers to a system which when it is booted up automatically executes a predetermined program for the user without instructions from the user.

Twenty Milliamp Loop

See Current Loop.

U

UART

This stands for Universal Asynchronous Receiver Transmitter. It is an integrated circuit for converting data from a parallel form to a serial form for transmission and vice versa when receiving data.

Underflow

The result of a mathematical operation which is too small for the computer to store. In some instances an error message may result.

USART

This is a Universal Synchronous Asynchronous Receiver Transmitter. An integrated circuit very similar to a UART but capable of sending data either synchronously or asynchronously.

User

The person who is using or operating a computer system or terminal.

User Orientated

A system is said to be user orientated if it can be easily used without a great amount of computer knowledge.

Utility Program

A program which forms part of the system software, written to perform tasks which are commonly used.

V

Variable
A quantity represented by a name or mnemonic which may be varied according to data entered into the computer or an expression which defines it.

VDU
See Visual Display Unit.

Virtual Memory
A system of using a small primary memory and a large secondary one to look as though they are a large primary memory. This is done by swapping data into and out of the primary memory whilst still addressing it as though it were a large primary memory.

Visual Display Unit
A unit used for displaying information from a computer. A VDU will normally incorporate a keyboard so that a two-way information transfer can take place. Often several VDUs will be linked to one computer.

Volatile
This refers to a type of memory in which the data is lost if the power to the system is switched off.

V24
See RS232.

W

Wait State
A state in which a processor is not executing an instruction. This often occurs when awaiting data inputs.

Winchester
A hard disk technology in which the heads take off and land when the drive is switched on and off on a specially reserved section of disk surface which is lubricated. In common with other hard disk technologies the heads "fly" a few micro-inches above the surface of the disk. Other hard disk technologies withdraw the heads so that they never touch the surface of the disk even when the power is removed.

Word
A unit of data consisting of a set number of bits. There are usually one or more bytes to a word.

Word Processor
A program for entering text into a computer, storing it, editing it and then printing it onto paper. Word processing packages have sophisticated editors which enable documents, letters, etc. to be easily entered into the computer and processed so that they can be printed out in the correct format.

Wraparound
The automatic continuation of one line onto the beginning of the next when the end of the first is reached.

Write
To transfer data onto a storage medium such as a disk or tape.

Write Protect

To protect a file or disk from having data written onto it. This is done in order to prevent wanted files from being over-written and lost.

Z

Zero Suppression
To remove the leading zeros in a number, i.e. the zeros to the left of the significant figures.

Zone
An area of memory reserved for a particular function.

BASIC
Reference Guide

In this section most of the common BASIC commands and functions are outlined. As different manufacturers will have their own particular form of BASIC there will be differences between one microcomputer and another. The terms in this reference guide have been included in the form in which they are most commonly found.

The commands for machine control, tape cassette control and disk control have not been included here because they do not form part of the BASIC language. In addition to this they vary too widely between different microcomputers for them to be usefully included here.

ABS
This function returns the absolute value of a number.

     50 Y = ABS(X)   is equivalent to $Y = |X|$

ASC
This function will take the decimal value of the ASCII code representation of the first letter within a string. (*See* Appendix 1)

     10 PRINT ASC("I")

prints

     73

ATN
This function returns the arc-tangent of a number for all real values.

     10 X = ATN(Y)

CHR$
This will generate a character from its decimal ASCII value.
(*See* Appendix 1)

    10 PRINT CHR$(73)
prints
    I

COS
This will return the cosine of the angle measured in radians.

    20 X = COS(Y)   Units of Y are radians

DATA
Items within a data statement may be numbers or string
characters if they are placed within quotes. They are read in
order by one or more READ statements within the program.

    10 DIM A$(10)
    20 DATA 1,2,5,"ANSWER IS "
    30 READ A,B,C,A$
    40 LET D=A+B+C
    50 PRINT A$;D
prints
    ANSWER IS 8

DEF
This statement enables the user to define functions within
the program. These functions take the form FN name (variable).

    10 DEF FNA(B)=B*100   function to multiply
        :   number by 100
    60 LET C=1·9
    70 LET D=FNA(C)   multiplies C by 100

DIM
Using this statement storage area within the computer
memory may be reserved for arrays or strings.

10 DIM A(20,5,6)	specifies a maximum size for array A of $20 \times 5 \times 6$
20 DIM A$(50),B$(10)	specifies a maximum length of 50 for string A$ and 10 for B$

A DIM statement is normally placed at the beginning of a program, but in any case it must be placed before the array or string which dimensions are used. In many computers there are default values for strings or arrays and below these lengths a DIM statement is not required.

END
This denotes the physical end of the main body of the program and execution is terminated when this statement is encountered. Subroutines or other sections of the program to which there are branches using a GOTO statement may follow on END statements.

EXP
This function returns the natural exponent of a number.

   100 Y=EXP(X)   this is equivalent to $Y=e^X$

FOR
The FOR statement causes any statements between it and its associated NEXT statement to be repeatedly executed. It takes the form:

```
FOR I=J TO K STEP M
   :
   :
NEXT I
```

The STEP command may be omitted if the default step of +1 is required.

```
10 FOR X=1 TO 20
20 PRINT X
30 NEXT X
```

This would cause the numbers 1 to 20 to be printed to the screen underneath one another.

GET
This is a form of input function which accepts a single numeric character or string character from the keyboard. A return is not required as a terminator as with the INPUT statement.

10 GET X	takes a single numeric character from the keyboard
30 GET A$	takes a single string character

GOSUB
The use of this statement causes the program to branch to a subroutine at a specified line number. A RETURN statement at the end of the subroutine returns control to the statement following the GOSUB.

    100 GOSUB 2000
       ⋮
       ⋮

2000 PRINT X	a simple subroutine to
2010 RETURN	print the value of X

GOTO
This causes the program to branch to the line number specified in the GOTO statement.

    100 GOTO 300

IF
If the relation which is specified is true then the program will branch to a specified line number or the instruction quoted will be executed. If the relation specified is untrue the following statement will be executed.

    100 IF A=10 GOTO 900
    150 IF A=12 then B=C

70

In addition to = the following relational operators are normally permitted:

      <   less than
      >   greater than
    <=   less than or equal to
    >=   greater than or equal to
    <>   not equal to (sometimes # is permitted)

Boolean operators may also be used i.e., AND, OR, NOT.

    10 IF A AND B THEN C=D   A and B must both be
                                         true (i.e., not equal to 0)

INPUT
The INPUT statements enables data to be entered during the running of a program. Each entry has to be terminated by return.

    50 INPUT X   this accepts the value of X
                            entered from the keyboard
    200 INPUT Y,A$ this accepts the value firstly of
                            Y then A$ from the keyboard

INT
This function returns the integral part of a number. In all cases $INT(X)$ is less than or equal to X.

    100 PRINT INT(5·4),INT(−5·4)
prints
    5   −6

LEFT$
This is used to return the left-hand section of a string. It takes the form LEFT$(A$,N) where N characters from the left-hand end of string A$ are returned.

    10 A$="123456789"
    20 PRINT LEFT$(A$,2)
prints
    12

LEN
This function returns the current length of a string.

    10 A$="ABCDEFG"
    20 PRINT LEN(A$)
prints
    7

LET
The LET statement enables a value to be assigned to a variable. For most microcomputer systems the LET statement is optional and may be omitted.

    70 LET A=B
    80 X=Y

The following arithmetic operations may be carried out:

    +   addition
    −   subtraction
    *   multiplication
    /   division
    ↑ or ^   exponentiation
    ( )   brackets to ensure order of evaluation

    40 Z=Y+X
    50 Z=(Y+X)*C/A

LOG
This function returns the logarithm to the base ten of a number.

    60 Y=LOG(X)

MID$
This function is used to return the middle section of a string and takes the form MID$(A$,M,N) where N characters from string A$ are returned starting at position M.

```
10 A$="123456789"
20 PRINT MID$(A$,3,3)
```
prints
345

NEXT
The next statement marks the end of a for LOOP – *see* FOR
statement.

ON
The ON statement is used in conjunction with either a
GOTO or GOSUB to conditionally branch to one of several
places.

```
110 ON A GOTO 1000,2000,3000
```

The rounded and intergerised value of A causes the program
to branch to line 1000 if A is 1, 2000 if A is 2, 3000 if A is 3
and so forth. The GOSUB option is used in a similar manner
for selecting a branch to a subroutine.

PEEK
This function returns the value of the memory location
designated by its argument.

```
100 Y=PEEK(928)        Y takes the value of the
                       data at location 928
```


POKE
Using this routine data can be entered into a specified memory location. It takes the form POKE address, data.

```
150 POKE 16223,13      data having the value 13 is
                       entered into location
                       16223
```


PRINT
This statement is used to print variables, expressions and
text to the screen. If more than one item is to be printed by

one PRINT statement then each item must be separated using a separator. If the separator used is a comma then the next item printed will start at the next preset tab position on the screen. These tab positions are determined by the internal software within each computer, and will vary from one type of computer to another. If a semicolon is used as a separator then no spacing will be given between the two items. Text should be enclosed between inverted commas.

```
10 X=10
20 Y=30
30 Z=50
40 PRINT "NUMBERS ARE ";X,Y,Z
```
prints
NUMBERS ARE 10   30   50

READ
This statement assigns data from a DATA statement to the variables within the READ statement in order. Numeric and string variables may be intermixed as shown below.

```
10 DATA 10,"ABCDEF",9,"HIJKL"
20 READ X,A$,Y,B$
```

REM
The REM statement allows a remark or comment to be entered into the listing. Anything following the REM is ignored by the program. Remarks are very useful as reminders of what a particular line or section of the program performs.

RESTORE
This statement resets the pointer for reading data from DATA statements to the first data item.

RETURN
A RETURN statement marks the end of a subroutine and causes the program to branch to the instruction following the GOSUB used to call the subroutine.

RIGHT$
This function returns the right-hand portion of a string. It takes the form RIGHT$(A$,N) where the last N characters are returned from string A$.

        10 A$= "123456789"
        20 PRINT RIGHT$(A$,3)
prints
        789

RND
This function returns a pseudo random number between 0 and 1.

        10 Y=RND(X)

Although the argument of the function X is basically meaningless it acts as a "Seed" and different values of X will change the pseudo random number sequence.

SGN
This function derives the sign of a number, i.e.

        SGN(X) is +1 for X>0
                   0 for X=0
                  −1 for X<0

SIN
This function returns the sine of an angle measured in radians.

        10 Y=SIN(X)

SPC
The SPC statement is used within a PRINT statement and takes the form SPC(N) where N spaces are printed.

        100 PRINT X;SPC(10);Y   ten spaces are printed
                                   between X and Y

SQR
This function returns the positive square root of a number greater than or equal to zero. An error message will be given if the number is less than zero.

    70 Y=SQR(X)   this is equivalent to
$$Y=\sqrt{X}$$

STEP
This is used within a FOR statement – *see* FOR statement.

STOP
This command stops execution of the program.

STR$
This string function converts a number to its equivalent string representation.

    100 A$=STR$(9·11)   A$ takes the value 9·11

TAN
This function returns the tangent of an angle measured in radians.

    30 X=TAN(Y)

VAL
This function takes a string containing a number and converts it to a numeric value.

    10 A$="9·11"
    20 X=VAL(A$)   X takes the value 9·11

If the string is not numeric then VAL(A$) will normally take the value 0.

Appendix 1

Table of ASCII Codes

ASCII code		Keyboard	Function
Hexadecimal	Decimal		
00	00	CTRL @	NUL
01	01	CTRL A	SOH
02	02	CTRL B	STX
03	03	CTRL C	ETX
04	04	CTRL D	EOT
05	05	CTRL E	ENQ
06	06	CTRL F	ACK
07	07	CTRL G	BEL
08	08	CTRL H	BS
09	09	CTRL I	HT
0A	10	CTRL J	LF
0B	11	CTRL K	VT
0C	12	CTRL L	FF
0D	13	CTRL M	CR
0E	14	CTRL N	SO
0F	15	CTRL O	SI
10	16	CTRL P	DLE
11	17	CTRL Q	DC1
12	18	CTRL R	DC2
13	19	CTRL S	DC3
14	20	CTRL T	DC4
15	21	CTRL U	NAK
16	22	CTRL V	SYN
17	23	CTRL W	ETB
18	24	CTRL X	CAN
19	25	CTRL Y	EM
1A	26	CTRL Z	SUB
1B	27	CTRL [	ESC
1C	28	CTRL \	FS

Table of ASCII Codes continued . . .

ASCII code Hexadecimal	Decimal	Keyboard	Function
1D	29	CTRL]	GS
1E	30	CTRL ^	RS
1F	31	CTRL __	US
20	32	Space	SP
21	33	!	!
22	34	"	"
23	35	£ or #	£ or #
24	36	$	$
25	37	%	%
26	38	&	&
27	39	´	´
28	40	(	(
29	41	)	)
2A	42	*	*
2B	43	+	+
2C	44	,	,
2D	45	−	−
2E	46	.	.
2F	47	/	/
30	48	0	0
31	49	1	1
32	50	2	2
33	51	3	3
34	52	4	4
35	53	5	5
36	54	6	6
37	55	7	7
38	56	8	8
39	57	9	9
3A	58	:	:
3B	59	;	;
3C	60	<	<
3D	61	=	=

Table of ASCII codes continued . . .

| ASCII code | | | |
Hexadecimal	Decimal	Keyboard	Function
3E	62	>	>
3F	63	?	?
40	64	@	@
41	65	A	A
42	66	B	B
43	67	C	C
44	68	D	D
45	69	E	E
46	70	F	F
47	71	G	G
48	72	H	H
49	73	I	I
4A	74	J	J
4B	75	K	K
4C	76	L	L
4D	77	M	M
4E	78	N	N
4F	79	O	O
50	80	P	P
51	81	Q	Q
52	82	R	R
53	83	S	S
54	84	T	T
55	85	U	U
56	86	V	V
57	87	W	W
58	88	X	X
59	89	Y	Y
5A	90	Z	Z
5B	91	[	[
5C	92	\	\
5D	93	]	]
5E	94	^	^

Table of ASCII codes continued . . .

ASCII code			
Hexadecimal	Decimal	Keyboard	Function
5F	95	—	—
60	96	`	`
61	97	a	a
62	98	b	b
63	99	c	c
64	100	d	d
65	101	e	e
66	102	f	f
67	103	g	g
68	104	h	h
69	105	i	i
6A	106	j	j
6B	107	k	k
6C	108	l	l
6D	109	m	m
6E	110	n	n
6F	111	o	o
70	112	p	p
71	113	q	q
72	114	r	r
73	115	s	s
74	116	t	t
75	117	u	u
76	118	v	v
77	119	w	w
78	120	x	x
79	121	y	y
7A	122	z	z
7B	123	{	{
7C	124	|	|
7D	125	}	}
7E	126	~	~
7F	127	Del	Del

Appendix 2

Table of Control Codes

NUL	Null (blank)
SOH	Start of header
STX	Start of text
ETX	End of text
EOT	End of transmission
ENQ	Enquiry
ACK	Acknowledge
BEL	Bell – audible
BS	Backspace
HT	Horizontal tab
LF	Line feed
VT	Vertical feed
FF	Form feed
CR	Carriage return
SO	Shift out
SI	Shift in
DLE	Data link escape
DC1	Device control 1
DC2	Device control 2
DC3	Device control 3
DC4	Device control 4
NAK	Negative acknowledge
SYN	Synchronous idle
ETB	End of transmission block
CAN	Cancel
EM	End of medium
SUB	Substitute
ESC	Escape
FS	File separator
GS	Group separator
RS	Record separator
US	Unit separator
DEL	Delete

Notes

Notes

Notes

Notes

Please note following is a list of other titles that are available in our range of Radio, Electronics and Computer Books.

These should be available from all good Booksellers, Radio Component Dealers and Mail Order Companies.

However, should you experience difficulty in obtaining any title in your area, then please write directly to the publisher enclosing payment to cover the cost of the book plus adequate postage.

If you would like a complete catalogue of our entire range of Radio, Electronics and Computer Books then please send a Stamped Addressed Envelope to:

BERNARD BABANI (publishing) LTD
THE GRAMPIANS
SHEPHERDS BUSH ROAD
LONDON W6 7NF
ENGLAND